Landing on the Other Side

A Book Of Poetry

Daryl Ross Halencak

LANDING ON THE OTHER SIDE

Printed in America

ISBN-13:978-0692301388 (BlaqRayn Publishing Plus)
ISBN-10:0692301380

Printed by Createspace 2014
Published by BlaqRayn Publishing Plus 2014

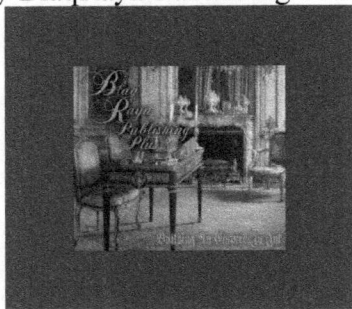

Edited by: **Julie C. Vigna**

List of Content

LANDING ON THE OTHER SIDE

Landing on the Other Side

LANDING ON THE OTHER SIDE

DEDICATION

This book is dedicated to:
Jane Hendrick Halencak, my wife and beloved
strength;
Edwina Halencak Fairchild, my mother;
Jean Halbert, my favorite high school teacher.

LANDING ON THE OTHER SIDE:
INTRODUCTION

"Does a poet living in West Texas understand his gift?"
How else to ask the question.

Words flowing onto the canvas of paper,
clutching the magic wand,
changing the blank sheet into Scripture,
creating pictures for the mind,
composing song and dance, and laughter and pain for the
soul.
Never really a loner is the poet,
just a sojourner on a foreign island
full of ghost people, visible and unseen;
listeners who wish to share the quest.
Apparitions never seeming real until they heard the voice.
After searching for the medium of expression,
this poet landed on another plain,
another, more comfortable reality.
This time, the habitation of my choosing — poetry.

This book chronicles the journey
of an itinerant poet finding a lush island.

Join me, as I share the wonder of *poetic words*.

LANDING ON THE OTHER SIDE

ROLLING PLAINS

I am a poet of the Rolling Plains of Texas.

I chronicle days, dreams, varmints, wastelands.

I write poems touching hearts, ushering change.

I pen verses making grown men cry and bastions crumble.

I rest among the needles of cactus.

My soul ascends to the flowering crepe myrtle:

soft, sweet, supple, like a mother's breast.

In the snow of winter, I lament prayers

from a pained heart.

Within the storms of sleet, Heaven appears elusive.

Then comes the spring; and I revel in the marvels

of the mating calls,

the building of nests, the abundance of seeds.

I am a poet.

I fly to the ends of the universe.

My passion has no limits.

DISTANT MOUNDS

In the distance, one can see the Medicine Mounds;

hear the silent cries of suffering women and children

murdered at the hands of marauding troops

assembled to capture the Chief.

He is nowhere to be found.

He has traveled far from the Pease River in search of bison.

Nomads, gathering wild plums and edible plants to sustain

hungry bellies, are easy targets for rifles.

Thundering horses attack.

The stench of death is the dark pall under the West Texas

sky.

The taste of fear clouds the sandy banks of the river bed.

Swords of genocide have ended the cleansing

of the small band of women and children,

huddled at the edge of the flowing, red, Pease River.

MY PEASE RIVER FRIEND, WILBUR

His name was Wilbur,

but everyone called him *Drunk*,

White Trash,

or just *Hey, You.*

Wilbur drew his last breath inside a rat-infested dwelling.

Alcohol fulfilled God's will.

The bootlegger was found curled, lying in his excrement.

He had slaked his drink of cheap elixir.

He died alone, with only his addiction to comfort him.

On the bed was a half-spent pint of rotgut,

clutched like a child's teddy bear.

He once owned a teddy bear — in his childhood dreams.

TIME SET APART: AT HOME BAKERY

I slip away, when I can, to Paradise.

This is the place of serenity in the centre of simplicity.

Sipping on a cup of freshly brewed coffee,

eating a warm homemade muffin.

Listening to jazz in the background,

friends surrounding on blue leather sofas.

The weather, politics, and rural life discussed here at Home.

Cherishing this oasis away from the cares of the day,

even if it is for an hour,

as embracing another peaceful sojourn at the local bakery.

A TRIP THROUGH THE POOL GARDEN

I take a walk around my pool-yard
on the first crisp afternoon of Fall —
only three hundred steps around that crystal sea of
blue.

Smelling the fresh fragrance of mint,
walking with bare feet,
stepping onto the green carpet
bordering my personal lake;
drinking the aroma and tasting juleps, tea.

Witnessing the wild salvia
waving its red flowers
as I passed by —
the first time noticing
the smiling plant in all of its
brilliant beauty.

The flora and fauna community grinning
honoring each plant: Asian jasmine,
holly, and desert sage.
The air clouding with the smells and sounds of the
menagerie.

LANDING ON THE OTHER SIDE

The statuary praying,
bowing awe to the garden.
St. Christopher winking at me.
Jude extending his protection to the garden.
Fiacre surveying his growing kingdom;
and the Virgin, holding the
garden's Sacred Heart.

Orange and golden
cannas swaying in time
to the music of the breeze,
tickling the wind chimes
of the leaves.

I was drawn into the pool,
walking on the holy waters
the garden gleefully nodding.
I was christened
by the love nature extended to me
on my prayerful pilgrimage
in the pool-garden.

LANDING ON THE OTHER SIDE

HAIKU: WEST TEXAS IN SUMMER

Ripe gourds and yucca

Tasting scent of baby's breath

Creeping Crepe Myrtles

Glowing smile and you

Sunshine filling sweet face, glory

Your green eyes blazing

Red soil, breaks shimmer

Comanche hills towering

West Texas on fire

Kissing of life, taste

Dirt roads blowing sandy loam

Parking at night, 'neath moon

LANDING ON THE OTHER SIDE

Saturday night sky

Grilling steaks, sizzle, mesquite steam

smells of my hometown.

LANDING ON THE OTHER SIDE

THE BREAK OF DAY

The soul treads the misty lane at daybreak,

seeks the sun's rays; it finds the center.

It's in the starry place within the quietness of the new day;

the scent of dew consumes its palate.

The sight of mourning doves cooing echoes the earth's

chant;

the towering loft of the ancient pecan tree has given rest

to the creatures of the garden.

All is good for Heaven's creation at this time of morning.

The softness is inhaled down to the core of the spirit.

The changing hues of the enveloping sky inspires

the soul to seek grandeur

in the unfolding new life of pastel blues.

I wait, facing the east, expecting my soul to return

full of brightness,

I am not disappointed.

LANDING ON THE OTHER SIDE

HAIKU: CONTEMPLATION UPON THE SUMMER ROLLING PLAINS

Do not disturb me

I tread the holy ground

The Pease has called me

Sacred soil, christened

Alone with the dried river

Immersed in peace, bliss

Tilled, worked, sweat, promised

Time stands still within my soul

Meditation, rest

LANDING ON THE OTHER SIDE

CHEESEBURGERS AND FRIES

My favorite burger temple never disappoints.

This country boy *done good* with his sacred manna:

Texas-style, for hungry bellies.

The joint feels like the Mountain bible story of the five

loaves and fishes on the Rolling Plains.

Grandmothers and high-schoolers dig into the Wednesday

nights.

Beans and cornbread:

meals fit for the king,

or red-necks,

or the Methodist preacher.

The pickups and Cadillac's

and bikers

and scooters

wait the long lines for Monday dinners.

Come one, come all to the gathering place, the Dairy Bar.

THE MARGARET METHODIST CHURCH

Souls made professions of faith

Dripping waters ran down the faces

as sins were washed away in the font.

Babies christened.

Young girls married young men.

Old men were blessed before the trip

to the *Great Beyond.*

Social Holiness marched out of the building

into the hurting hearts and hungry bellies.

LANDING ON THE OTHER SIDE

HALLOWEEN ON MAIN STREET

Fright night, moon's bright canopy of orange

covered the munchkin marauders

Main Street was filled with ghosts, ghouls

and fairy princesses

Corn candy meted out by the handful

Sounds of laughter, moans of terror sounded

throughout the neighborhood

Shadows-chased boogeyman hid behind every

dark bush and tree.

Crisp air shrouded the excitement

of the Hallowed Eve

In my hometown.

LANDING ON THE OTHER SIDE

CHOP WEEDS, CLEAN THE POOL,
ON MAIN STREET USA

I began my routine weekend of

grubbing weeds and mowing the manicured lawn,

Saturday chores

resulting in spiritual fulfillment.

I drove my pick-up truck to Vernon and Wichita Falls

to garner the supplies required to maintain my pool.

Parties, and weekend just hanging out, are

awaiting with anticipation.

Neighbors and guests alike attending with memo pads; to

write

what they observed — the good, the bad and the occasional

weed.

They observe to determine my state of mind —

they know that if my yard is perfect,

then I am contented with life; and found Enlightenment,

at least for today.

UNTITLED

When I pass, I will have no requests

The blaze will only consume the chaff

I will devise and bequeath the bounty

Of the Harvest of the Universe

Ashes to ashes

When I go to glory land

Will God smile for me?

THE PICTURE

I am the canvas of the landscape.

Paints are the beauty of God.

The clouds of the picture are my thoughts.

Sunrises radiate from my eyes.

The soul poses for the artist like a grain of sand

whirling in the midst of the Dust Bowl.

The gaze of my world sees green pastures,

faces of sunflowers

wheat berries

My legacy reflects the painting of the field of my life.

the picture, the poise
the strength of my existence
wait for the review

LANDING ON THE OTHER SIDE

GHAZAL: THE GREAT DEPRESSION, FOARD COUNTY, TEXAS

And the huddled masses raise their fists in prayer.

And the huddled masses raise their fists in prayer.

Hungry stomachs cried out peasants' alarm.

And the huddled masses raise their fists in prayer.

The greedy robbed bread from mothers' arms.

And the huddled masses raise their fists in prayer.

Wall Street power brokers spread wide their charm.

And the huddled masses raise their fists in prayer.

Migrant workers picked cotton on white man's farm.

And the huddled masses raise their fists in prayer.

Outsourced jobs stole our dreams, created harm.

And the huddled masses raise their fists in prayer.

HOME SWEET HOME

Dysfunctional families sit around a Norman Rockwell

spread.

Eating the perfectly burnt Thanksgiving turkey dinner;

planning the Christmas meal,

before digesting the banquet set before the gathering obese.

A mile away,

street people, suffering from Agent Orange,

cuddle together for warmth.

Bellies full of nothing cry for mercy,

while the cranberry sauce is passing around the hall.

Candles lighting, proclaiming *Peace on Earth.*

At Thanksgiving —

No peace, when children are killed

with switchblades and meth.

Pipes are passed, and disillusioned

fall into the oblivion under the street lamps.

Happy Holidays

LANDING ON THE OTHER SIDE

excluded the tired,

the poor masses.

Yes, celebrate *Good Will on Earth* during the season of

Hope

within this land of *no*.

TORNADO ALLEY

Southwestern clouds rolled onto the dry plains, ushered in

hurricane force winds.

The Heavens appeared like a swirling mix of brown,

grey and green

as Mother Nature prepared her assault.

The Death Angels focused their telescopic sights on rural

villages and suburban cul-de-sacs. Scanning the horizon,

families observe the voodoo talismans announcing the time

for entrance

into underground shelters.

Those without root cellars or concrete bunkers huddled

together in disheveled interior closets.

Most filled with children's clothes and Sunday go-to-

meeting suits hanging on wooden rods.

Interior shelters proved to be flimsy protective mantillas,

covering the cowering family.

LANDING ON THE OTHER SIDE

Fears grasped the residents; like the clutches of circling
hawks

to unprotected rodents.

And then, like the ominous blast in Nagasaki, it hits.

It hits with a fury, with anger and malicious intent.

Once on the ground, the sound of a freight train crashing

into a brick wall.

Metal sheets wrapped around ancient buildings, like

Christmas tinsel hung from a Christmas tree.

Semi-trucks thrown around like baseballs at a little league

game.

There is no game here; only destruction and death.

Bloody bodies tossed about within the storm's funnels.

Homes with families inside — leveled.

Mighty trees collapse onto the underground shelters.

Even those cloistered within the earth are neither safe, nor

saved.

LANDING ON THE OTHER SIDE

The gods of the skies had their way, as the world watched

the drama — played out on the Weather Channel.

LANDING ON THE OTHER SIDE

WHERE PLANTED

At the edge of the once flowing Pease River, I am planted

along with the cottonwood trees.

Through my staring eyes, my ancestors stood on the same

spot

on this river bank: admired nature,

noticed the mottled cottonwoods from the sandy loam,

dreamed this young sapling

would grow into clouds above the homestead;

provided shelter to traveling cardinals,

held the shifting sands in the predestined place;

caused the twirling winds to sing as wisps of air brushed

across the green leaves,

provided welcome sounds to vagabonds;

spotted fishing holes,

tasted the waters seeping into thirsty ground.

Generations admired this growing cottonwood,

LANDING ON THE OTHER SIDE

marveled at its determination to survive,

smiled as they watch the solace of the tree's strength.

It surrounded the pioneer family;

birthed, grew, expanded for over one hundred years.

I am one of the cottonwoods' trustees: also loving my river,

cherish the flora and fauna canopied

by my cottonwood

continued to mature,

looked at this turret, enveloped by other cottonwoods

surviving the ages,

gave sustenance to this hallowed land and its peoples.

Yes, here I planted.

THE CENTER OF TOWN

The social life of this small town

happens in a place among cotton swabs and prescriptions.

Between rows of men's underwear and greeting cards,

cough syrup and Tylenol.

Grumpy old men and hired hands

gather around tables and chairs,

with seats well-worn by those dropping by for a cup

of coffee and discussions.

Men debating issues of the local high school;

or who deserves to sit in the Oval Office,

can be heard from corner to corner of the pharmacy.

Friendship takes on a special meaning

for the regulars, from early morning until five o'clock,

when the sidewalks are rolled up and stored for another

day

at Shaw's Pharmacy.

FIELDS OF WHEAT HAY

The homestead dies on the vine.

Cloudless skies, over 100 degrees,

tanning the leathery, fried skin of working field hands —

the owners of the dirt patch call it *Home Sweet Home.*

Swirling dirt filling the lungs, and

life sapping rays scorch the cracked mud clods.

The cotton, what is left of it — chopped.

Useless wheat straw bales of hay — stacking for winter

feeding

of skin-and-bone cows.

Petitions light the darkened rooms of working man and

woman.

Mournful cries rise toward heaven,

as the sun grants no mercy.

HOLY SAINT FRANCIS, PRAY FOR HER

Evening.

As the street lights dimly shine,

the kitten crawled out to feast on the bugs.

Huddled in the middle of the thoroughfare,

she cautiously searched for sustenance.

The stray looked in horror as vehicles sped by,

oblivious to her presence.

One morning, the stray appeared at my office door.
Allowed inside, she stayed,
and became entrenched in my heart.

Now, a fixture;

a celebrity of Main Street,

peers from her glass court —

looks over her subjects.

She gives thanks to St. Francis.

GRANDMOTHER'S HOME GARDEN

Death nourishes sky-drenched earth.

Discarded rind decomposes.

Green scavengers crowd the mound.

Canna lilies encircle mounds of green.

Worms till wet soil.

Ants harvest Mother's bounty.

Wild peas serve nutty flavor.

Rosemary fills the air.

Yucca pricks the rendered bounty.

Soft grass caresses tender toes.

Crunching sounds near.

Sweet surrender fills the soul.

SUNDAY LUNCH

Sunday — lunching on baloney sandwiches.

TV trays replacing formal settings.

Gone forever are tables draped in starched linens,

white-shirted males wearing

paisley neck ties, hanging down to the navel.

Family togetherness replaced by mindless zombies

watching the Dallas Cowboys or the OKC Thunder;

or, God forbid, the golf game live from Pebble Beach.

Stories passing down from generation to

generation by the blue-haired ladies and the ear-haired

elders.

Yes, forever losing the magic, the sacredness of Sunday

lunch.

DETERMINATION

She was never called *physically handicapped.*

She was "only a mother and farmer's wife".

College was challenging, but not an obstacle.

Neither was getting pregnant,

when the community discouraged it.

Mother overcame Polio with true grit

and the absence of pity.

Willed to be strong,

she was an example for all survivors.

LANDING ON THE OTHER SIDE

SOLDIERS OF HUMANITY

All around they see sorrow

and hear unsettling cries.

Soldiers wait for a tomorrow,

yet they see humanity die.

Hearts thirst, yet time is wasting.

The war calls far from home.

Young sons slake wine for tasting.

Only blood they drink alone.

Souls shrouded in soiled carpets.

Wars fought for oil and gain.

Spiraling funds and rising market.

Septic tears, vile substitute for rain.

All around us see their sorrow,

hear unsettling cries.

LANDING ON THE OTHER SIDE

Our soldiers waited for tomorrow,

only to feel their humanity die.

THE BLOWING PIONEERS

They — saddling the bucking winds

blowing sands

tumbling the weeds

rolling down the plains

sailing — with

the sun blazing parched skin

bathing the ocean of pioneers with the waves of sage

the drought smelling the fury

as the wagon trailed the open stretch of dirt —

our people were calling for a home; with thirsting

hearts and dreaming minds

for sanctuaries —

Yes, Paradise.

GHAZAL: THE RURAL POOR

Tonight, I will dine on the banquet of sorrows and grief.

Tonight, I will dine on the banquet of sorrows and grief.

Huddled masses live on the street in despair.

Tonight I will dine on the banquet of sorrows and grief.

Greedy lion pounces on the poor from the lair.

Tonight, I will dine on the banquet of sorrows and grief.

The soul of humanity seeks what is fair.

Tonight, I will dine on the banquet of sorrows and grief.

The earth cries for healing and repair.

Tonight, I will dine on the banquet of sorrows and grief.

Starving families ask the one percent to share.

Tonight, I will dine on the banquet of sorrows and grief.

The world turns, no one cares.

Tonight, I will dine on the banquet of sorrows and grief.

LANDING ON THE OTHER SIDE

A SULTRY WEST TEXAS NIGHT

Dry, salty sand covers undulating bodies.

Naked toes clutch the red dirt, while the earth trembles

underneath.

The bonfire and *shit-kicking* tunes fill the air with

excitement.

Breezeless, full-mooned canopy hides the torrid abandon.

Morning dawn, parents turn blind stares to the three o'clock

return.

Sunday morning gives its attention to young farmers

still in high school,

after another Saturday night.

LANDING ON THE OTHER SIDE

LOOKING TREE

Looking Tree stares at the stars.

Planted on the banks of the Pease River,

Looking Tree does not dare move from that holy shore.

Immobile by its own choice is the Looking Tree.

Feeling Bush holds the shifting sand in the deserted
homestead.

Located far from the banks, time blows the land.

The holy soil feeds the resilient scrub.

Immobile by its own choice is the Feeling Bush.

Cool Wind captures the chiming of the autumn leaves.

Looking Tree and Feeling Bush sway as autumn nips.

Prayers float to the glowing moon for Solstice Light.

Immobile by its own choice is the Cool Wind.

LANDING ON THE OTHER SIDE

Autumn Death prays for its next victims.

Lashing tongue can taste the next meal.

Immobile by its own choice is Autumn Death.

GHAZAL: AND THE RIVER RUNS DRY TODAY

And the river runs dry today.

And the river runs dry today.

Thundering clouds, blistering heat.

And the river runs dry today.

Dreams of clover, soft and sweet.

And the river runs dry today.

No more sorrow, cycles complete.

And the river runs dry today.

West Texas needs moisture for cattle and wheat.

And the river runs dry today.

THE DIRT FARMER

The dirt farmer bleeds sweat into his planted fields.

The cotton withers within the red clay soil.

The dirt farmer prays for a good crop —

enough of a yield to support his family.

But he knows that *Wall Street* and

city boys control the price of his harvest.

He is a slave to the great, bowtie-adorned

masters run the local co-op.

He is indentured to commodity boards located

far away from his piece of *Heaven*.

In spite of the grave obstacles,

in spite of the physical torture, the grueling labor,

he remains a believer in the American dream,

because he served his country well

when the draft board came knocking on his door.

He paid taxes to the best of his abilities.

He pledged allegiance to the flag

under which he was born.

He is devoted to the concepts of equality, regardless

of ethnic identity, or religion or class.

Draped by such values, he desperately tries to understand

and to stand strong

— and, yet —

he utters unto himself when no one is listening —

"Is there really One Nation Under God, with

Liberty and Justice for All?"

In the dead of his sleepless nights, he questions his dogma.

In times of his economic woes, when he has

trouble putting food on the table,

he cries out.

No one hears his feeble, shaky voice.

The dirt farmer searches for the promised economic

justice for all —

the core belief in the true pursuit of happiness.

LANDING ON THE OTHER SIDE

But,

how can one be happy with hungry bellies?

Unpaid bills? Artificially low crop prices?

He remains a devoted, card-carrying American,

even though his heart of hearts reminds him that

his country has abandoned the family farmers.

He is told by the politicians, that

"in the Land of the Free and the Home of the Brave",

capitalist principles will win; and

the war against family farmers will cease.

The end of the market-driven struggles will arrive

when the market corrects itself.

All will be well with the world —

So they tell the dirt farmer.

DINO

He sneaks.

He creeps.

He pees on the couch and I do not care.

With soft steps,

masking twenty-five pounds

covering a massive frame, he tears apart my soul.

White fur, blue eyes, devious expressions,

Angel stalker captures both my heart and my home.

He pounces with sharp fangs and angry claws

aimed at the unsuspecting trespasser onto his domain.

Night hunter.

Lap dancer at my desk, or my chair, or my bed,

LANDING ON THE OTHER SIDE

His split personality loops from angel to demon.

Blue eyes glow, observe with unearthly instincts.

I taste the salty smell of his breath, and I can smile.

He summons with purrs, relaxes with undulating

movements.

I am haunted by his eyes, fascinated by his demeanor,

loved by his distant affections.

LANDING ON THE OTHER SIDE

AS IS THEIR RIGHT

The dream has faded

into the sunset for the family farmers.

On the other side of the mountain, however,

Wall Street flourishes: with

its golden parachutes;

and its bailouts;

and its perks.

Back to the homestead, houses foreclosed;

The workers and farmers

and the oppressed have heard the

clarion call for true democracy,

and for economic equality.

They shall, as *One*, rise up to partake from the table —

as is their right.

JANE'S SMILE

Among the flowering Crepe Myrtle I wandered

Lantana covered the soil

I tasted the scent of Baby's Breath

And thought about your green eyes

And glowing smile.

I SEE HEAVEN

Heavenly Sky is spattered onto the eternal canvas with hues

of blues and reds, never grey.

The walking heights praying before us, with lifted

loincloths

of western clouds.

The Universe expresses Spirit with dripping sweetness and

delight.

Flowers breathe deeply and inhale

Eyes with praise gaze thereupon

and

Spirit minions give glory.

Hills and foothills gladly sing.

And I smile.

LANDING ON THE OTHER SIDE

LOVE

I was ten years old when my grandmother died.

My parent sat at her side for months in that rural

hospital.

My sister and I did not understand.

Mother could not explain.

My father also waited by her side.

He made a decision to forego his planting.

He missed that year's cotton planting

at the vigil.

He loved his beloved mother-in-law.

STARS AND BARS IN THE BREEZE

Not a pretty picture

traveling down dirt roads,

gazing at waving stars and bars

flying over white trash shanty towns.

Fabric couches on the porch in the rainy afternoon.

War flags of the Old South displaying on broken-down

pick-up trucks.

Bob Wills playing loudly on Saturday nights.

Epitaphs shouting with hate.

rot-gut beer flowing down red-necked throats.

JESUS SAVES, or so the preacher's telling on Sunday

morning.

Hung-over congregation waiting for Dallas Cowboys.

Monday morning bringing the early trip to work,

accompanied by Rush Limbaugh on the radio.

Yes, they love West Texas and Jesus.

LANDING ON THE OTHER SIDE

MY FREEDOM, MY REDEMPTION

I was a child to no one …

… not cancer, not a stroke, not M.S.

I arrived at the house named *Wholeness*.

I traveled the street called *Freedom* …
… no longer captured by a society of greed.
No need for robber-baron railroads.
I entered the *Land of Milk and Honey*.

I, stressed by nothing …

… painted my portrait in my own blood,

not the grey-skinned cripple,

colored with the pain of my ancestors.

The walls crumbled down.

I traversed the mountain trail to my rebirth —

and I have safely completed that journey

to wellness and completion.

LANDING ON THE OTHER SIDE

ESCAPE

Respecting the dark within,

I graciously allow this hound to chase me through my yard.

I have no choice.

My talents capture him in the snare.

The black shadow continues to pursue me.

I escape its lethal, crushing bite.

Learn to smile as the demon snaps my ankle.

This poet is freeing himself from the deadly grip.

Curiously chronicle its trailing,

as he sniffs the blood trail

left by his wounded casualty.

I escape the snare.

LANDING ON THE OTHER SIDE

MODERN SCIENCE

I.

This poet stands in the exam room

Alone …

Naked …

Scared …

Piercing eyes of caretakers examining.

Thoughts of death nesting.

Mentally escaping solitary confinement,

in a cancer–ridden body.

Remembering childhood days,

Carefree ...

Healthy ...

Existence being full of good times remembered.

Health is just a surgery away.

LANDING ON THE OTHER SIDE

II.

There I was, in the crypt of fate's design,

ensnared in the cobweb of tubes,

in orifices created just for me.

Stapled.

Sewn.

Morphined.

Monitored.

The techno-world watched from every angle

as the *Angel of Death* hovered,

clutching the life.

Life support has an explosive meaning

when one has cancer.

I wanted that black widow out of me.

I fought to be free

from her vampire lair.

III.

Stab the knife deep within the damaged flesh.

Release the impure elements of the soul to immortal

dimensions.

Cry out for times past —

Scream loudly … scream proudly.

Don't waste time — allow the scabs to heal.

Stab the knife deep within damaged flesh.

Yes, release the impure elements of the soul to immortal

dimensions.

IV.

Entrails removed

and wrapped in saline-soaked gauze,

after the body is torn asunder

LANDING ON THE OTHER SIDE

and ripped wide open.

I lie there unaware of the trauma inflicted.

the cancer is to be removed.

The life-force is threatened by the procedures to save.

I suffered in silence — suffered alone.

And, as if a miracle occurred,

I lived thereafter

and faced another day.

LANDING ON THE OTHER SIDE

SMOKE

I.

Marlboro smoke spiraling

into darkness;

contemplating.

Sitting in the breezeway,

confused by the morrow's demands.

Dreaming of escape,

envisioning freedom

from the Puritan work ethic;

satisfying, like the black soot filling his lungs.

II.

On the porch in the dark,

LANDING ON THE OTHER SIDE

Staring at the billowing curls of smoke

ascending upward as I exhale.

Taking another puff.

Drawing it deep down into the body.

Visualizing the toxins entering the blood stream.

The lungs gasping for pure, sweet oxygen.

I am a cancer survivor.

I am slowly doing my system harm.

Yet, I draw in another breath of toxins.

LANDING ON THE OTHER SIDE

HIS HEART ATTACK

Gasping breath, failing lungs; his world ended

— or so it seemed.

He slipped into unconsciousness,

time after time,

until the *EMTs* arrived

Deep within the *grey matter*,

he worried that someone would pull the plug prematurely.

Somehow, he endured.

With tingling toes, and legs without strength;

He tried to stand — he could not move.

His nose smelled the death-stench of

dying man.

His mouth tasted the bitter bile welling up inside.

His chest felt crushing pain.

LANDING ON THE OTHER SIDE

He heard the ribcage crack —

Like lightening striking a dry field.

Pain worse than the living funeral pyre.

Throughout the ordeal,

his forlorn family cried out for mercy.

His children sent up prayers,

like balloons released at a birthday celebration.

And as if God heard the pleas:

Petitions granted. Miracles happened.

Yes, a celebration, indeed —

Death was cheated once more.

LANDING ON THE OTHER SIDE

THE NEW JERUSALEM

Dedicated to President Barack Obama

I.

Rainbow hues of skin.

No bell-curve of age.

All were one

Somberly waiting,

Longing for the new day of hope.

II.

Alas, we were spat upon

By the irreligious church folk.

Elitists threw stones

III.

And then —

Powers and principalities buckled.

Bridges built.

Walls fell.

Rubble cemented by unity,

into New Jerusalem.

WHEN WOODY GUTHRIE COVERED THE SKY

He was *Emissary of Unity*, healed the cleave,

Trudged barefoot into love.

Built bridges across the chasm created by conflict.

The breach between men could not remain once he spoke.

He was *Ambassador of Social Justice*.

The disenfranchised took up the full cup.

He gleefully laughed and offered a refill.

Refugees of war and famine entered his tent,

opened wide for all.

He took hold of a hammer, and broke the glass ceiling.

He was representative of the best of humanity.

Hues and shades of his fabric blended into brightness.

Woody's spirit marched in Selma,

kicked down the Rio Grande wall,

LANDING ON THE OTHER SIDE

lay down between the lamb and the lion

— and the universe smiled.

LANDING ON THE OTHER SIDE

THE FALLEN

The lives were not lost in vain

Excellence was virtue

Valor was its pride

The lives were not lost in vain

Through years of toil in the Middle East

Hardship and stress never dampened the resolve

The lives were not lost in vain

The *Ancient of Days* watched their families

Traditions upheld their souls

The lives were not lost in vain

LANDING ON THE OTHER SIDE

Homage owed to the fallen

Loyalty is given to each

And we bow in reverence, because —

The lives were not lost in vain

LANDING ON THE OTHER SIDE

GINSBERG

HOWL! Those who have ears,

let them hear.

Beat it out

and the social agenda will be changed.

Scream at the top of your lungs

and the powerful Wall Street

bastions will crack,

like mirrors in the presence of island sirens.

Run up the street

and conquer the *Citadel of the Damned.*

Even if we tarry,

know we are crossing the moats.

Arrows cannot pierce the words of resolved hearts.

LANDING ON THE OTHER SIDE

Risk it all, like Allen did

and then we can smirk.

BARBED WIRE BED

Inspired by *Bonhoffer*

I am lying on a bed of nails.

Clotting blood is oozing onto the rusty spikes.

The pain shoots like flowing

lava from a spewing volcano.

Barbed wire violently caresses my neck.

The ancient strand of fencing is encrusted with maggots,

feasting on the pooling blood.

The wire tightens around my neck.

The nails crucify my body.

Life is drained, choked by the designs of my own creation.

THE LIVES OF GUS

Within the nocturnal bewitching hours, he died

a thousand deaths…this man named Gus.

Each night, he awaited his execution; or his impaling,

or his crucifixion.

Gus is never prepared for these regular battles.

The Angel of Death smiled in anticipation of the eminent

slaughter.

Gus prepared for war with his internal demons.

His sleepless hours scramble his mind, as do the

uncontrollable

lucid dreams.

Each night, the same ending.

None too soon, arrived the dawn; as Gus died in his nightly

dreams,

and found resurrection

in the misery of his workday toils.

LANDING ON THE OTHER SIDE

He woke covered in the stench of fear … the screams

of putrid blood gushing from his lungs.

His days filled with morbid curiosity of his demise.

He determined the nightly bouts.

During the day, Gus dressed in a pinstriped suit,

or in prisoners' neon orange, or a contractor's overalls.

Gus was each of us.

LANDING ON THE OTHER SIDE

CLARA

I met Clara after her stay at the asylum.

She takes an emery board to her wrist and imagines

nirvana.

Dark shadows encircle her life

like the mascara painting her eyes.

Glass chards are her passion.

She visualizes swallowing needles from her

mother's sewing basket.

She cries for help —

Nothing.

THE LIFE OF A POET

quills dipping in ink

hands shaking from excitement

the master, feeling the smooth blank page

smiling with the face of a genius

an obscure novice

a budding wordsmith

impregnating, with the wisp of wisdom and insight

flowing like the Nile

creation floating, belly-up

basking in the shining rays of deep thought

transubstantiating into the moment

silent laughter

griping stern expressions

the life of a poet — scary, but wonderful.

LANDING ON THE OTHER SIDE

HEAVEN'S PORTAL

I.

Death.

Gazing up,

scanning the horizon

for the hand of the *Infant*,

I flounder like a fish, in the primordial ooze enveloping me

waiting for the sound of fluttering wings.

My Guardian Angel must arrive, or I will drop from

Existence

into the vast Nothingness.

Smelling my own fear — it tastes of bile.

Listening to my silent cries — I am disgusted.

Landing On The Other Side

Are these the whimpers of a man without faith?

Perhaps I am in *Purgatory*.

Molding and rotting on this altar of my own creation.

II.

They appear — yes! My guardian and the *Infant!*

Michael in all of his glory. Yes, Archangel Michael,

my Beloved, the *Holy Infant of Prague*,

dropping Jacob's Ladder.

LANDING ON THE OTHER SIDE

FORGIVENESS

I must learn to forgive myself.

It is in forgiving that I can find the love of others.

I regret putting my own pain aloft the suffering of those I
love.

The temple on the mountain of selfishness is a lonely
citadel.

I must learn to forgive myself.
It is in forgiving that I can appreciate the love of others.
Perceiving threats destroy the *Oneness* of kindness.
The temple on the mountain of selfishness is a lonely
citadel.

I must learn to forgive myself.

St. Francis being my example in love and self-respect.

Teaching to preach love, to both the creatures of the earth
and the enemies.

The temple on the mountain of selfishness is a lonely
citadel.

A LIST COMPOSED ON A RAINY SUNDAY MORNING:

The Reflections of a Man From The Back Pew

I make a few opinions from the back pew:

Reverence is not reserved for the sanctimonious;

All who are holy are not sanctified;

Grace is not the prized possession of a chosen remnant;

The grave does not release the few with angel

wings and harps on the day they call *The Rapture;*

The *Amen* corner often frequents the saloon;

The doors and Eucharist must be open to all.

LANDING ON THE OTHER SIDE

OUR LADY

My Beloved beckons me: *Come and feel my sacredness.*

She tells me that in the Beginning was the Word;

warm to the touch, honey to the palate.

I heed her call: *She is the Poem of the Spirit, the aroma of*

spring.

Her Blessed realm of light lures to the portal;

tender as the breasts of Angels,

fertile as the Womb of the Virgin.

I am drawn forward: *I step into the hallowed crevasse.*

I arrive on the plains of divinity.

I hear the liturgy of the poetic chants.

I swirl into higher consciousness, by my Enchanted Lady.

I step through the Icon of Poetry.

I feel my soul, nurtured by Her graces.

THIS BEAST OF MINE

I am the one captured within the belly of the beast.

I took my time choosing the correct whale, the exact one.
I wanted to entomb my soul.
Well, maybe not entomb; let us just say,
the one with whom I wanted to
spend the rest of my life.

This one, that swallowed me whole?
Poetry.

THE CRITICS

They told me my works are the same in theme and content:

too dark and depressing.

"Heaven seems so far removed from life, your prose and

poetry."

I have been advised to chronicle the pure,

the beautiful, the pleasant.

Readers prefer pulp fiction.

The mass consumers will

appreciate my works,

if I paint faux smile —

I do not listen.

LANDING ON THE OTHER SIDE

"Show that milk-white, Sunday School persona, hidden

somewhere deep down,"

has been their sincere request.

Request denied.

I will write what I feel; and as long as the words have

meaning to me,

the words will flow.

I am content with my expressed words,

even if they are dismissed.

LANDING ON THE OTHER SIDE

HAIKU: IN THE HIGH DESERT GARDEN,

MARATHON, TEXAS

I sojourned into this bucolic garden, high into the Big Bend
area.
I gazed. I looked. I tasted. I wrote. I smelled.
I became one within the beauty of nature.

Fountain softens skin

High mountain breath fills dry lungs

Coolness, my cocoon

Delicate flowers

Sequestered pool, spent foliage

Birds mouth prayers, awe

Pregnant pollen clouds

Desert skies fill hungry plants

Orgasmic prayer

LANDING ON THE OTHER SIDE

Clouds cloister the shade

Salvia slakes on damp banks

Nesting beds of soil

Sheathed in toughened green

Ants harvest Mother's bounty

Worms till dank soil

Male homage, a gift

Receptive to the warming

Moments of life, lived

Engage the marvel

Lips of birds gently taste sap

Tongues touching sweet joy

IN THE LAND OF MILK AND HONEY

The mutt had such a sad and pathetic look,
dodging pick-up trucks
living on the dirt road where she was abandoned
eating road kill to survive
unwanted pups cluster around the mother,
like flies on excrement.
Sounds like the unwanted waifs and disenfranchised,
living the American dream.

LANDING ON THE OTHER SIDE

VESPERS

Total quietness engulfs,
as I read my favorite books of poetry.
I lift, as a priest raises the *Host* towards Heaven.
My mind transubstantiates into the worn paperback.
We become *One* as I comfortably recline into my favorite
easy chair.
Socked feet dangle and toes wiggle to the beat of my
favorite
Byzantine CD.
My essence is kneeling in waist-high waters
awaiting my baptismal christening into the sacred writ.
My mind wanders, and ponders the written word —
thoughts
thunder through my head, like a West Texas storm.
Sacred revelations flood my soul.
My sojourn from the television is well worth the time.

THE POETRY OF LIFE

I.

Entwine my heart, rapturous whirlwind, in ecstasy of pure

spirit.

Carry me to my undeserved reward in the here and now.

Sequester my loins in the blowing twirls on Mount Zion,

until I come face to face with the King of higher thought

and knowledge.

II.

Naked I was born, and naked I shall die,

until I am clothed in your righteousness and your artistry.

Toughen my hands; strengthen my arms like the forged

steel

of your powerful thoughts,

and I shall accomplish great things for you.

III.

Teach me your ways and I shall create silvery mountains,

glistening underneath the sun of your glory.

I shall take my place clothed in the shade, as you instruct

with the radiant beauty of knowledge and power.

Show me your arts, and I shall paint the ceiling of your

skies.

Shepherd, lead the way; and I shall follow you into the

valley

of your resting place,

to join your throng of enlightened beings.

IV.

I must learn the tools you have placed by my side;

and I continue to write this unfinished, poetic rhapsody.

LANDING ON THE OTHER SIDE

POETS

Edgar Allen, I felt your soul when you said, *I have not
seen
as others saw...*
My spirit cried as I read Andrew M. Scott's lament: *I
prowl
in my cage...*
Paradise does not appear in my rear-view mirror;
as I travel down the lonely narrow path, predetermined
by my *Lord.*
I sojourn alone; watching my feet on my personal
yellow brick road,
as I ring around and around in my sequestered,
circular labyrinth.

My brothers, I experience your individual ways,
even though you did not choose your path.

LANDING ON THE OTHER SIDE

FACES

Faces.

I awakened in the witching hour of the night.

The room was dark.

The glow from the street light crept through the curtains.

I saw silhouettes encroaching on the bedchambers

As the room embraced its own persona

I crawled out of bed, and headed for a beer to appease

the internal demons

As I walked toward the kitchen, past the furniture, I noticed

the shadow of a man.

It was I.

Staring into the mirror, I noticed that I am not alone.

I recognized them.

I looked at the ghosts of my past.

Noted that ourselves in the reflection peered back.

I saw the myriad of souls giving definition in that moment.

LANDING ON THE OTHER SIDE

Faces of wonder. Hopeful.

Fearful; solidly in the present moment.

Turning around, I smiled at them.

I looked into the faces of the embryos of my future.

CONTACT THE AUTHOR

To arrange for a speaking engagement with
Daryl Ross Halencak, email him at
artist@srcaccess.net

CONTACT THE ARTIST

Artist Contact Information
artist@srcaccess.net

ABOUT THE AUTHOR

Daryl Ross Halencak of Crowell, Texas is author of "Landing on the Other Side", "Staring Blue Eyes", and "Poetry, Passion, Life". He is a 2011, 2012, 2013 and 2014 Woody Guthrie poet in Oklahoma.

He is a nationally and internationally recognized poet and has been a featured reader in Oklahoma, Texas, California and New Mexico venues. His works are published in both America and the Czech Republic. Halencak is the Foard County Attorney , who is a fifth generation resident .

"Landing On the Other Side" leads the reader through a real sense of place, times and heroes in the North Texas part of Texas: rugged, untamed, compassion and diverse. The excursion through the Rolling Plains evokes the true abilities of survivors. And, the poet knows too well of being a survivor. His works pen the steadfast spirit of North Texas.

Author Daryl R. Halencak

Books By Daryl R. Halencak

Staring Blue Eyes

Poetry, Passion and Life:

A Collection of Poetry and Haiku

WILD IVY GROWS

The ivy twines up the prison wall.

It speaks to this political prisoner, chained within cloistered

walls.

The green growth makes the activist smile, as

he anticipates his firing squad, or injection.

The vivid color of the wild ivy

infuses his dreams;

gives the symbol of the living,

though he will not be alive for long.

He sends prayers from his tortured heart to believers of *The*

Faith.

This comrade will be united with the bride of his passions.

In the meantime, he dreams of Utopian life, as he admires

the ivy growing up the wall.